AS YOU THINKETH

by JAMES ALLEN

Revised and Updated
by Dr. Tag Powell

Top Of The Mountain Publishing
Largo, Florida

AS YOU THINKETH
The Inspirational, Motivational Classic
by JAMES ALLEN
Revised and Updated
by DR. TAG POWELL

Hardcover ISBN 0-914295-68-3
Trade ISBN 0-914295-69-1

Copyright 1988 by Dr. Tag Powell

Printed in the United States of America
Library of Congress Cataloging-in-Publication Data.
Allen, James
As You Thinketh.
1. New Thought.
I. Powell, Tag.
II. Title.
BF639.A48 1988   158'.1   88-12347

Top Of The Mountain Publishing
11701 S. Belcher Road, Suite 123T
Largo, Florida 34643 U.S.A.
(813) 530-0110 SAN 287-590X

You hold in your hands one of the greatest books of all time.

This little giant could have been called by many titles:

"The Handbook for Higher Living," for it holds some of the true answers for the enjoyment of life and successful living;

"The Book of Vibrant Health," for it gives you the true cause of good health, and how to obtain it;

"The Book of Instant Enlightenment," for it explains the real Laws of the Universe, and the secrets of how to make these Laws work for you—now.

You might even call this work "The Book of Answers," for it covers everything from: how to lose weight to reaching the top of the achievement ladder; how to overcome circumstances to increasing your visions and ideals. Apply the techniques of this book, and they will change your life for the better.

As You Thinketh has been updated and revised—using easy-to-read, modern-day language—by one of the nation's top, human potential trainers, Dr. Tag Powell.

You will read this book in about a half hour, and you will use its dynamic thoughts for the rest of your life.

Time spent enjoying *As You Thinketh* is an investment in your future:
"It will be the first half hour of the BEST of your life."

YOU ARE

AS YOU THINKETH.

TABLE OF CONTENTS

Special thanks to Neal Storrs, Ph.D.,
for his help in revising and editing.

Original Illustrations
by Kae Campbell

Optimal Reading

Type-size, leading and column-width
were selected for maximum reading
speed and maximum comprehension,
researched by
The Speed Reading Institute.

FOREWORD

This little volume (the result of meditation and experience) is not intended as an exhaustive treatise on the much-written-upon subject of the power of thought. It is suggestive rather than explanatory, its object being to stimulate men and women to the discovery and perception of the truth that:

"They themselves are the maker of themselves"

by virtue of the thoughts which they choose and encourage; that Mind is the master weaver, both of the inner garment of character and the outer garment of circumstance, and that, as they may have hitherto woven in ignorance and pain, they may now weave in enlightenment and happiness.

James Allen

Mind is the Master-power
   that molds and makes,
And you are Mind
   and evermore you take
The tool of Thought, and,
   shaping what you will,

Bring forth a thousand joys,
   a thousand ills:
You think in secret, and
   it comes to pass,
Environment is but
   your looking-glass.

Thought and Character

...so does your every act spring from the
hidden seeds of your thoughts.

THOUGHT
AND
CHARACTER

The saying, "As you thinketh in your heart so are you," not only covers every facet of your existence, but is so comprehensive that it reaches out into every aspect of your life. It is really true that *you are what you think*— your personality is the complete sum of all your thoughts.

In the same way that a plant grows from its seed, so does your every act spring from the hidden seeds of

...you...contain within you, the ability to
transform into anything you wish.

your thoughts. This is true not only of those actions that are done deliberately, but also of actions taken spontaneously and without planning.

Act is the blossom of thought: joy and suffering are its fruits. In this way, you cultivate and reap the sometimes sweet, sometimes bitter harvest of your gardening.

You are created, and then grow according to fixed laws—not by whim. Cause and effect are as absolute and unchanging in the hidden realm of thought as they are in the visible world of material things. An upstanding, God-like character does not come about by luck or chance, but is the result of a continued effort of right thinking; that is, the effect of long cherished association with God-like thoughts. For the same reasons, a low, animalistic character is the result of continually thinking evil, undesirable thoughts.

You are made or unmade by you alone. You can either forge the weapons by which you destroy yourself, or fashion the tools with which you build your heavenly mansion of peace, strength and joy. By the right choices, and true applications of thought, you ascend to Divine Perfection; by abusive, wrong habits of thought, you descend below the level of the animal. You are maker and master of your thoughts. Between these two extremes lie all the shades of character. It is up to you to determine where, in that spectrum, you will fall.

Many, beautiful truths concerning the soul have been brought to light in our era, but none is more joyous, or full of divine promise, than this one: You are the master of your thoughts, the molder of your character, the maker and shaper of your environment and your destiny.

As a being of Power, Intelligence and Love, and the lord of your own thoughts, you hold the key to every situation, and contain within you, the ability to transform into anything you wish.

You are always master, even in your weakest, most downtrodden state. But in your weakness and degradation, you are like a foolish master who misgoverns his or her "household." You must think hard about your situation, and strive to return to the foundation upon which your being is constructed, before you can again, become a wise master who acts in the "household's" best interest. The only way to become such a master is to discover, within you, the laws which govern thought, and this discovery can only be accomplished through experience and careful self-analysis.

Only through much searching and mining are gold and diamonds obtained. You can find every truth connected with your being, if you will dig deep into the mine of your soul.

For only by...ceaseless effort can one enter
the door of the Temple of Knowledge.

For in the mine of your soul, you will discover that you are the maker of your character. Through similar exploration, you can find every truth connected with your inner self—how you are the maker of your character, the molder of your life, and the builder of your destiny. You will see yourself shaping your own thoughts, watching their effect on you and on others, using every event that occurs in your life, no matter how trivial, as a means of obtaining that knowledge about you which is Understanding, Wisdom and Power.

Here, more than in any other area of your life, is the absolute Law that, "Those that seek, find; and to them that knock, it shall be opened." For only by patience, practice and ceaseless effort can one enter the door of the Temple of Knowledge.

Effects of
Thought on
Circumstance

Your mind may be compared to a garden,
which can be intelligently cultivated, or
allowed to run wild.

EFFECTS OF
THOUGHT ON
CIRCUMSTANCE

Your mind may be compared to a garden, which can be intelligently cultivated, or allowed to run wild. However, regardless of whether the mind is cultivated or neglected, it will produce fruit. If no useful seeds are planted in the garden then an abundance of useless weed-seeds will fall into place, and from these will grow nothing but weeds.

Just as a gardener cultivates his plot of land, keeping it free from weeds, and growing the flowers and fruits which he desires, so should you tend the garden of your mind, weeding out all wrong, useless and undesirable thoughts; cultivating to perfection the flowers and fruits of right, useful and pure thoughts. By pursuing this process, you will, sooner or later, discover that you are the master-gardener of your soul, the director of your life. You will also discover within you, the laws of thought, and understand more clearly how thought-forces and mind-elements operate in the shaping of your character, circumstances and destiny.

Thought and character are one. The outer conditions of your life will always be in harmony with your inner state. This does not mean that your circumstances, at any one moment, are an indication of your entire character; however, your outer circumstances are intimately connected with some vital thought-elements within you that, for the time being, are indispensable to your development.

You are where you are now by the law of your being. The thoughts which you have built into your character have brought you here. In the arrangement of your life there is no element of chance; instead, everything is the result of an absolute, unchanging law. This is just as true of those who feel "out of sync" with their surroundings as of those who are contented with them. As a progressive and evolving being, you are where you are so that you may learn: that you may grow. And as you learn the spiritual lesson which any circumstance holds for you, this episode passes away and creates a void for other circumstances.

You are ruled by your outer circumstances only as long as you believe yourself to be a creature of outside conditions. The moment you realize that you have creative power, and that you control the hidden soil and seeds from which your outer

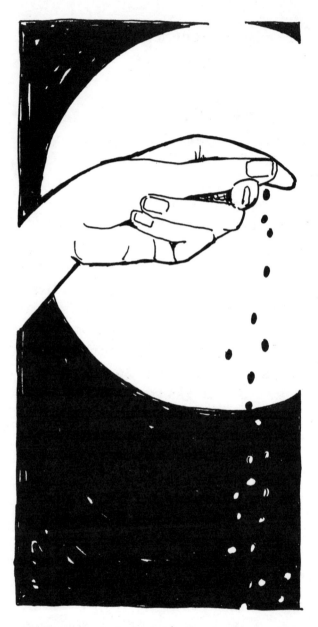

Any thought-seed which falls into the soil of the
mind...produces its own offspring....

conditions grow, you then become the rightful master over YOU.

Anyone who has practiced self-control and self-purification under-stands that circumstances *grow out* of thought, for they know that every change in their condition has been connected to a change in their mental state. For they will have noticed that the alteration in their circumstances has been in exact ratio with their altered mental condition. There is one further proof of this truth: As soon as you make real progress in correcting the flaws in your character, you pass rapidly through a series of changes in your personal environment.

The soul attracts that which it secretly harbors, those things it fears, as well as those things it loves. It soars to the heights of its most cherished aspirations, and sinks to the level of its basest desires. Circumstances are the projections of the soul's inner thoughts.

25

Any thought-seed which falls into the soil of the mind and takes root, produces its own offspring, which sooner or later, blossoms into a harvest of actions, circumstances and opportunities. Good thoughts bear good fruit, bad thoughts bear bad fruit.

The outer world of circumstance shapes itself to the inner world of thought. Pleasant and unpleasant external conditions make for the ultimate good of the individual. As the reaper of your harvest, you learn both by suffering and happiness.

By following one's innermost desires, hopes and thoughts—whether in pursuing the will-o-the-wisps of impure imaginings, or steadfastly walking the highway of strong and noble endeavors—individuals, at last, arrive at their fulfillment in the outer conditions of their lives. The same laws of growth apply everywhere.

A person does not come to drugs, alcohol, poverty or prison because of fate or circumstance, but by traveling the path of impure thoughts and desires. Nor does a pure-minded person fall suddenly into a world of crime because of outside forces. Criminal thoughts must have led a secret existence for a long time in the heart, waiting for their hour of opportunity to burst forth. Circumstances do not make or shape you; they reveal you to you. No one ever sinks into vice without an inclination toward negative behavior; nor does anyone ascend into pure happiness without cultivating virtuous thoughts. You, therefore, as the lord and master of your thoughts, are the maker of you; the creator, shaper and author of your environment. Starting at birth, and along every step of its earthly journey, the soul attracts those conditions which reflect its own purity and impurity, its own strengths and weak-

Your thoughts and actions are what determine your fate...if impure they will imprison you....

nesses.

People do not attract that which they *want,* but that which they *are.* Their innermost thoughts and desires are fed with their own food—whether it is healthy or rotten. The "divinity that shapes our end" is within us. The only thing that handcuffs you is you. Your thoughts and actions are what determine your fate. If they are impure they will imprison you; if they are noble they will liberate you. You do not receive what you wish and pray for, but only what you truly deserve. Your wishes and prayers are only answered when they are in harmony with your thoughts and actions.

In the light of this truth, what, then, is the meaning of the phrase, "fighting against circumstances"? It means that you are constantly struggling to change your outer conditions, while at the same time feeding the *cause* of those conditions in your heart. That cause may be a conscious vice or an unconscious weakness. Whatever it is, it defeats your efforts to change your outer conditions, and thus, must be driven out.

Some people are anxious to improve their circumstances, but are unwilling to change themselves; they, therefore, remain imprisoned. Those, on the other hand, who do not shrink from self-sacrifice, will never fail to accomplish the purpose upon which their heart is set. This is as true of earthly as of heavenly things. Even those whose only goal is to acquire wealth must be prepared to make great personal sacrifices before they can accomplish their object.

Some people are miserably poor. They are extremely anxious to improve their home surroundings, but they avoid hard work, and believe that because they are paid little they are justified in trying to cheat their employer. Such people do not understand the simple principles which are the foundation of true prosperity. They are not only totally unfit to rise out of their misery, they actually attract to themselves an even deeper misery by behaving in lazy and deceitful ways.

There are rich people who are the victims of a painful, lingering disease called gluttony. They are willing to give away large sums of money to rid themselves of this disease, but they are not willing to give up their gluttonous desires. They want to gratify their tastes for rich, unhealthy foods, and keep their health as well. Such people are totally unfit to enjoy health, because they have not yet learned the primary principles of leading a healthy life.

There are employers who break the law in order to avoid paying their employees a standard wage so they can make a larger profit for themselves. Such persons are altogether unfit for prosperity. When they find

...the popular idea that you fail because you are
honest, or succeed because you are
dishonest, is simply not accurate.

themselves bankrupt, both in reputation and material wealth, they blame circumstances, not understanding that they alone are to blame for their condition.

I have introduced these three cases only to illustrate the truth that individuals are the authors of their own circumstances, although almost always without knowing it. While they aim at a good goal, they are continually preventing themselves from attaining it because of thoughts and desires which cannot possibly be in harmony with that goal. Such cases could be multiplied almost indefinitely. However, it would be more convincing if you, the reader, traced the actions of the law of thought in your own mind and life.

Circumstances are so complicated, thought is so deeply rooted, and the conditions of happiness vary so much from individual to individual, that one's soul-condition cannot be judged merely from the external facet of one's life. You may be honest in certain aspects of your life, yet suffer loss; you may be dishonest in certain situations, yet acquire wealth. But the popular idea that you fail because you are honest, or succeed because you are dishonest, is simply not accurate. When you have gained a deeper knowledge and wider experience, you will find such a judgment to be false. The dishonest person may have virtues which others do not possess; the honest person may have vices which are absent in others. Honest people reap the good results of their honest thoughts and actions; they also bring upon themselves the suffering which their vices produce. Dishonest people, likewise, cause their own suffering and happiness.

It flatters our vanity to believe that we suffer because of our virtues. But not until we have cast out every sickly, impure thought from our minds, and washed every sinful stain from our soul, can we be in a position to know that our suffering is the result of our good—and not of our bad—qualities. And long before we reach that supreme perfection, we will have found within our minds that Great Law which is absolutely just, and which cannot, therefore, give good for evil; evil for good. Possessed of such knowledge, we know that our lives are, and always have been, justly arranged, and that all our past experiences are the rightful results of our evolving selves.

Good thoughts and actions can never produce bad results; bad thoughts and actions can never produce good results. In other words, nothing but corn can come from corn, nothing but sandspurs can come from sandspurs. Many people understand this law in their normal, everyday lives, and work within it; but few understand it in the mental and moral worlds, though its operation there is just as simple and unchanging.

...nothing but corn can come from corn....

Suffering is *always* the effect of wrong thought in some direction. It is an indication that individuals are out of touch with themselves and with the Law of their being. The sole and supreme use of suffering is to purify: to burn out everything that is useless and impure.   Suffering ceases for those who are pure. There is no reason to burn the ore after the gold has been removed; by the same token, a perfectly pure and enlightened being could not suffer.

The circumstances in which you encounter suffering are the result of your own mental disharmony; the circumstances in which you encounter happiness are the result of your own mental harmony. Happiness, not material possessions, is the measure of right thought; unhappiness, not lack of material possessions, is the measure of wrong thought. You may be cursed and rich, or blessed and pure. Happiness and riches are

...as you change your thoughts toward your environment and other people, your surroundings and other people will change toward you.

blended together when the riches are wisely used. The poor only sink into misery when they believe their lives are burdens that have been unfairly imposed.

Poverty and ill health are the two extremes of misery. Both are unnatural and the result of mental disorder. You are not in your proper condition until you are happy, healthy and prosperous; and happiness, health and prosperity are the result of a harmonious adjustment of the inner you with your outer surroundings.

Humans only begin to be human when they cease to curse and complain, and start to search for the hidden justice which regulates their lives. From the moment you accept that truth, you cease to accuse other people and your surroundings, and begin to build within you, strong and noble thoughts. When you stop criticizing your circumstances, you start learning how to use them to achieve more rapid progress, and as a means of discovering the hidden powers and possibilities within you.

Law, not confusion, is the dominating principle in the universe; justice, not injustice, is the soul and substance of life; goodness, not corruption, is the moving force in the spiritual government of the world. Since this is the case, you must set yourself right in order to see that the universe is right. And in the process of setting yourself right, you will find that as you change your thoughts toward your environment and other people, your surroundings and other people will change toward you.

The proof of this truth is in every person, and it is, therefore, easy to investigate it through self-analysis. The minute you radically alter your thoughts, you will be astonished at the rapid transformation it will bring about in the material conditions of your life. Some people imagine that thoughts can be kept secret—they cannot. They quickly crystallize into habit, and habit solidifies into circumstance.

Animal thoughts crystallize into habits of drunkenness and excess, which harden into circumstances of misery and disease. Impure thoughts crystallize into unhealthy and confused habits, which harden into distracting and difficult conditions. Thoughts of fear and doubt crystallize into weak and indecisive habits, which harden into circumstances of failure, poverty and dependence. Lazy thoughts crystallize into habits of uncleanliness and dishonesty, which harden into circumstances of poverty. Hateful and judgmental thoughts crystallize into habits of accusation and violence, which harden into circumstances of injury and persecution. Selfish thoughts crystallize into habits of self-seeking, which harden into circumstances of misery.

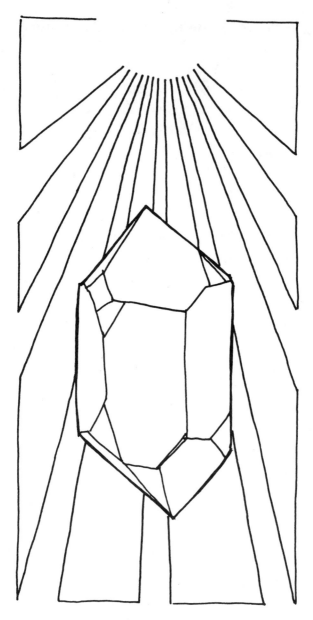

...beautiful thoughts of all kinds crystallize into
habits of grace and kindliness....

On the other hand, beautiful thoughts of all kinds crystallize into habits of grace and kindliness, which solidify into warm, sunny circumstances. Pure thoughts crystallize into habits of moderation and self-control, which solidify into circumstances of peace and calm. Thoughts of courage and self-reliance crystallize into vigorous habits, which solidify into circumstances of success, wealth and freedom. Energetic thoughts crystallize into habits of cleanliness and hard work, which solidify into circumstances of happiness. Gentle and forgiving thoughts crystallize into habits of gentleness, which solidify into protective and nurturing circumstances. Loving and unselfish thoughts crystallize into habits of forgetting oneself for the sake of others, which solidify into circumstances of pure and lasting prosperity and true riches.

A particular train of thought,

good or bad, if persisted long enough, cannot fail to have an effect on character and circumstance. You cannot *directly* choose your circumstances, but you can choose your thoughts; and so indirectly, you can shape your circumstances.

Nature helps everyone to reach the goal of their foremost thoughts, and presents opportunities which will quickly bring to the surface both good and evil thoughts.

From the moment you cease your negative thoughts, all the world will soften toward you, and be ready to help you. The world becomes your kaleidoscope, and the varying combinations of colors which it presents to you are the exquisite picture of your evermoving thoughts.

_____ Effects of Thought on Circumstance

Effects of Thought on Health and Body

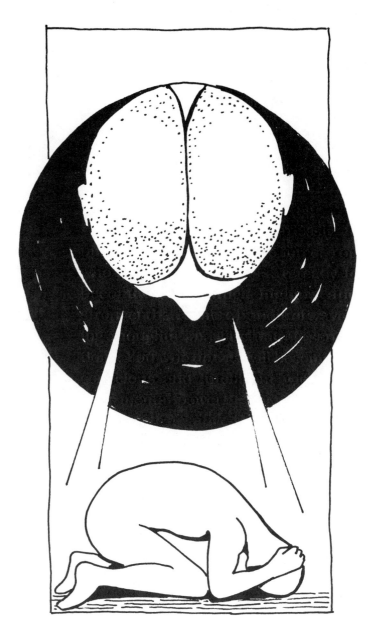

The body is the servant of the mind.

EFFECTS OF THOUGHT ON HEALTH AND BODY

The body is the servant of the mind. It obeys the operations of the mind, whether they are deliberately or instinctively chosen. When commanded by unlawful thoughts, the body sinks rapidly into disease and decay; at the command of beautiful thoughts, it becomes young and beautiful.

Disease and health, like circumstance, are rooted in thought. Sickly thoughts express themselves through a sickly body. Thoughts of fear have been known to kill as quickly as a bullet, and they are continually killing thousands of people every day just as surely, if less rapidly. People who live in fear of disease are the same people who get it. Anxiety demoralizes the entire body, and lays it open to disease. Impure thoughts, even if they are not physically indulged in, will soon shatter the whole nervous system.

Strong, pure and happy thoughts build the body in vigor and grace. The body is a delicate and pliable instrument, which responds readily to the thoughts which are then impressed.

People will continue to have impure and poisoned blood so long as they think unclean thoughts. Out of a clean heart comes a clean life and a clean body. Out of a corrupt mind comes a corrupt life and a corrupt body. Thought is the fountain of life; make the fountain pure, and everything will be pure.

Change of diet will not help you unless you change your thoughts. Purify your thoughts, and you will no longer desire impure food.

Clean thoughts make clean habits. So-called saints who do not wash their bodies are not really saints. Those who have strengthened and purified their thoughts would cleanse the body to shed the presence of dirt.

If you would perfect your body, guard your mind. Thoughts of malice, envy, disappointment and depression rob the body of its health and grace. A sour face does not appear by chance; it comes about because of sour thoughts. Wrinkles that spoil a youthful face are the marks of excessive passion and pride.

I know a woman of ninety-six who has the bright, innocent face of a girl. I also know a man not yet into

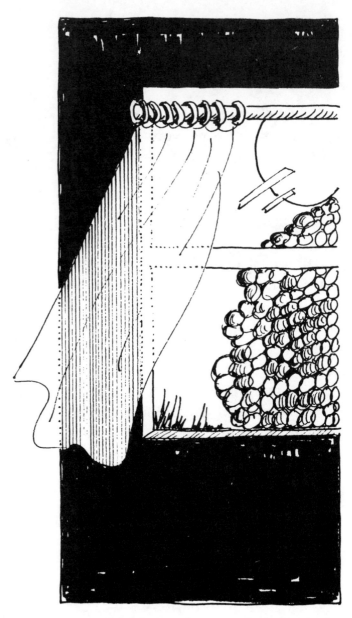

...you cannot have a clean, sweet-smelling home
unless you let air and sunshine into your
rooms....

middle age whose face is pinched and wrinkled. The first one is the result of a sweet and sunny disposition; the other is the outcome of passion and discontent.

Just as you cannot have a clean, sweet-smelling home unless you let air and sunshine into your rooms, so can your body be strong and your face bright and happy only if you fill your mind with thoughts of joy, goodwill and serenity.

On the faces of the aged there are many different kinds of wrinkles; some being the results of strong, healthy thought, while others being lines carved by passion. For those who have lived honorably, the process of aging is calm and peaceful, like the setting sun. I recently visited a phi-losopher on his death bed. He was old only in years, and died as sweetly and peacefully as he had lived.

There is no medicine like cheer-

...thoughts of peace toward every creature....

ful thought for curing the ills of the body, and there is no greater comfort than goodwill for dissolving the shadows of grief and sorrow. To live continually with thoughts of cynicism, suspicion and envy is to be locked into a self-made prison. But to think well of all, to be cheerful with everyone, to patiently seek out the good in everyone—such selflessness is the very essence of heaven. To dwell day by day in thoughts of peace toward every creature brings the joy of abundant peace.

Thought
and
Purpose

...people allow the ship of thought to drift upon the ocean of life.

THOUGHT
AND
PURPOSE

Until thought is linked with purpose there can be no real accomplishment. The majority of people allow the ship of thought to drift upon the ocean of life. Aimlessness is a vice, and if drifting is allowed to continue it will surely lead to disaster.

Those who have no clear purpose in their lives fall easy prey to petty worries, fears, troubles and self-pity. All these indications of weakness lead—just as surely as deliberate wrongdoing—to failure, unhappiness and loss.

You should formulate a legitimate purpose in your heart, and then set out to make it come true. You should make that purpose the focal point of your thoughts. It could be either a spiritual ideal or a material object, but whatever it is, you should make this purpose your supreme duty. Devote yourself to its attainment, and do not allow your thoughts to wander down side-roads of temporary longings and imaginings. This is the royal road to self-control and true concentration of thought. Even if you fail again and again to accomplish your purpose (as you must until weakness is overcome,) the *strength of character* gained will be the measure of your *true success,* and will form a new starting point for future triumphs.

Those who do not wish to undertake a *great* project, should fix their thoughts on the faultless performance of their day-to-day activities, no matter how insignificant those tasks may appear. Only in this way can their thoughts be gathered and focused, and determination and energy be developed. Think in this manner, and anything may be accomplished.

The weakest soul, knowing its own weakness, and believing this truth—*that strength can only be developed by effort and practice*—will at once begin to exert itself. Through patient effort, it will never stop developing, and will at last grow divinely strong.

As physically weak individuals can make themselves strong by careful and patient training, so can persons of weak thoughts make themselves strong by exercising themselves in right thinking.

Having decided on your purpose, you should
mentally lay a straight path to its achievement.

To put aside weakness and aimlessness, and to begin to think with purpose, is to join the ranks of those who see failure as another pathway to success; who make all conditions serve them, and who think strongly, attempt fearlessly, and accomplish masterfully.

Having decided on your purpose, you should mentally lay a straight pathway to its achievement, looking neither to the right nor to the left. Doubts and fears should be rigorously excluded. Thoughts of doubt and fear never accomplish anything, and never can. They always lead to failure. Purpose, energy and powerful thinking cease when in creep doubt and fear.

The will *to do* springs from the knowledge that *you can*. Doubt and fear are the great enemies of knowledge. You who encourage such feelings are your own worst enemy; you who have conquered doubt and fear have conquered failure. Your every thought brings new power, and all difficulties are met bravely and are successfully overcome.

Thought bonded fearlessly to purpose becomes creative force. You who already *know* this are ready to become something higher and stronger than a mere bundle of wavering thoughts and fluctuating sensations. You who *do* this will become the conscious and intelligent wielder of your mental power.

_____ Thought and Purpose

The Thought Factor in Achievement

...loss of balance would mean total destruction

THE THOUGHT FACTOR IN ACHIEVEMENT

All that you achieve and all that you fail to achieve are the direct result of your own thoughts. In a just universe, where loss of balance would mean total destruction, individual responsibility must be absolute. Your strength and weakness, purity and impurity, are your own, and not of another person; they are brought about by you, and not by another; and they can be changed by you, never by another. The situation you live in is also your own, and not of another person. Your suffering and your happiness are created from within. As you think, so are

You can rise, conquer and achieve only by
lifting your thoughts.

you; and as you continue to think, so shall you remain.

Strong persons cannot help the weaker ones unless the weaker are *willing* to be helped, and even then, the weaker persons must become strong on their own. They must, by their own efforts, develop the strength which they admire in others. Only they can change their condition.

In the past, people have usually felt that their lives were controlled by an all-powerful "Other," and they hated that person for controlling their lives. Now, however, more and more people are coming to understand that the truth is very different: People who feel controlled by another are in reality cooperating in their own enslavement. A wise person sees the law of nature at work in the weakness of the oppressed and the misapplied power of the oppressor; and, being compassionate, condemns neither.

When you have conquered

...they must lift their thoughts above slavish,
animal indulgence.

weakness, and put away all selfish thoughts, you belong neither to the class of oppressors nor of the oppressed. You are free.

You can rise, conquer and achieve only by lifting your thoughts. You can remain weak, miserable and groveling only by refusing to lift your thoughts.

Before individuals can achieve anything, even in the realm of worldly things, they must lift their thoughts above slavish, animal indulgence. They need not give up *all* kinds of selfishness, but at least a portion of it must be sacrificed. Individuals whose first thought is animal indulgence can neither think clearly nor plan methodically. They cannot find and develop their latent resources, and will fail in any undertaking. Not having learned to control their thoughts, they are not in a position to control their affairs and to take on serious responsibilities. They are not fit to act independently and stand alone. Remember, however, that they are limited by only one thing—their own thoughts.

There can be no achievement, no progress without sacrifice. The worldly success of individuals will depend on how much they are able to sacrifice their confused, lower, animal thoughts, and fix their minds on strengthening and developing their independence and self-reliance. The higher they lift their thoughts, the more upright and righteous they become, the greater will be their success, and the more blessed and enduring will be their achievements.

The universe does not favor the greedy, the dishonest and the vicious, although on the surface it sometimes appears that way. In fact, it helps the honest, the generous and the virtuous. All the great teachers of the ages have stated this truth in varying ways, and to prove it to yourself you need only strive to become more and more virtuous by lifting your thoughts.

Intellectual achievement is the result of thought dedicated to the search for knowledge, beauty and truth. Such achievements are sometimes motivated by vanity and ambition, but they are never the result of those characteristics. They are the natural outgrowth of long, hard effort, and of pure and unselfish thoughts.

Spiritual achievements are the consummation of holy aspirations. One who lives constantly in the realm of noble thoughts, who meditates upon all that is pure and unselfish, will, as surely as the sun rises at dawn, become wise and noble in character, and rise into a position of influence and fulfillment.

Achievement, of whatever kind, is the crown of effort and thought. By the aid of self-control, persistence, purity, principle and well-directed thought a person ascends. Through the effects of animalistic behavior, laziness, impurity, corruption and confusion of thought a person de-

Achievement, of whatever kind, is the crown of
effort and thought.

scends.

Individuals may rise to high success in the world, and even to lofty altitudes in the spiritual realm, then just as quickly, descend into weakness and mediocrity by allowing cocky, selfish and corrupt thoughts to take possession of them. Victories attained by right thought can only be maintained by watchfulness. Many weaken as soon as success is assured, and rapidly slide back into failure.

All achievements, whether in the business, intellectual or spiritual world, are the results of consciously directed thought. They are governed by the same law. The only difference between them lies in the *object of attainment.*

Those who seek to accomplish little need sacrifice but little; those who would accomplish much must sacrifice much; those who strive to attain highly must sacrifice greatly.

Vision
and
Ideals

The dreamers are the saviors of the world.

VISIONS
AND
IDEALS

The dreamers are the saviors of the world. As the visible world is sustained by the invisible, so are people, with all their trials and tribulations, nourished by the beautiful visions of their solitary dreamers. Humanity must not forsake its dreamers and their ideals, for their dreams are *realities* which will one day come to pass.

Composer, sculptor, painter, poet, prophet, sage—these are the makers of the after-world, the architects of heaven. The world is beautiful because they lived; without them, humanity would perish.

81

You who cherish a beautiful vision, a lofty ideal in your heart, will one day have it realized. Columbus cherished a vision of another world, and he discovered it. Copernicus had a vision of a multiplicity of worlds in a vast universe, and he revealed it. Buddha beheld the vision of a spiritual world of stainless beauty and perfect peace, and he entered into it.

Cherish your visions, your ideals, the music that stirs in your heart. Through them your world will grow more beautiful. And if you remain true to them, the ideal world of your dreams will at last be built.

To desire is to obtain; to hope is to achieve. Is it right that the lowest desires of an individual be gratified, while their purest hopes starve for lack of nourishment? No, for this is a violation of the Law: "Ask and receive."

Dream lofty dreams, and you

will become what you dream. Your Vision is the promise of what you will be someday. Your Ideal is the prophecy of what will one day be unveiled.

The greatest achievement was in the beginning, just a dream. The oak sleeps in the acorn; the bird waits in the egg; and, in the highest vision of the soul, an angel stirs. Dreams are the seedlings of realities.

Your circumstances may be difficult, but they will not remain that way if you focus on an Ideal, and strive to attain it. You cannot expand on the *outside*, and remain stagnant on the *inside*.

Imagine yourself a poor, young laborer; working long hours in a factory, and never being exposed to the advantages of education or culture. The moment you dream of better things—refinement, grace and beauty —you begin to see a better way of life. The vision of greater liberty takes pos-

Dream lofty dreams, and you will become what
you dream.

session of you. You begin to devote all your spare time and money to the development of your latent powers. Soon the factory becomes too small to hold you. You are so out of harmony with your old surroundings that you shed them as naturally as if you were taking off your coat. Imagine yourself years later, now fully grown. You are a master of the forces of your mind, through which you wield worldwide influence and almost unequaled power. In your hands, you hold the strings of great responsibility. You speak, and the lives of thousands are changed. Men and women hang upon your every word as, sun-like, you become the fixed and luminous center around which innumerable destinies revolve. You have realized the Vision of your youth. You have become one with your Ideal.

You, too, will realize the Vision of your heart, whether corrupt, beautiful or a combination of both, for you always gravitate toward that which

Into your hands will be placed the results of
your own thoughts.

you most love. Into your hands will be placed the results of your own thoughts. You will receive what you earn; no more and no less. Whatever your present environment may be, you will rise, fall or remain stagnant according to the power of your thoughts, your Vision, your Ideal. You will become as small as your controlling desire; as great as your dominant aspiration.

In the beautiful words of Stanton Kirkham Davis, "You may be keeping accounts, and presently you shall walk out of the door that for so long has seemed to you the barrier of your ideals, and shall find yourself before an audience—the pen still behind your ear, the ink stains on your fingers—and then and there shall pour out the flood of your inspiration. You may be aimless, misguided, and you shall wander to the city—confused and open-mouthed; shall wander under the brave guidance of the spirit into the studio of the

The thoughtless, the ignorant and the lazy...
talk of luck, fortune and chance.

master, and after a time, he shall say, 'I have nothing more to teach you.' And now you have become the master, who did so recently dream of great things while drifting and lost. You shall lay down the saw and the plane to take upon yourself the remodeling of the world."

The thoughtless, the ignorant and the lazy, seeing only the outer effects of things and not the things themselves, talk of luck, fortune and chance. Seeing a person grow rich, they say, "How lucky they are!" Observing another become knowledgeable, they exclaim, "How highly they are favored." And noting the saintly character and great influence of others, they remark, "How chance aids them at every turn." They do not see the trials, failures and struggles which these people have voluntarily encountered in order to gain their experience. They have no knowledge of the sacrifices they have made, of the courageous efforts they have put forth, of the faith that has sustained them along the path to the Vision of their heart. They do not know the darkness and the heartaches; they see only the light and joy, and call it "luck." They do not see the long, hard journey; they see only the rewarding goal, and call it "good fortune." They do not understand the process; they see only the effort, and call it "chance."

In all human affairs there is *effort* and there is *result,* and the strength of effort—not chance—is the direct cause of the result. Powers and possessions, whether material, intellectual or spiritual, are not "gifts," they are the fruits of effort. They are thoughts completed, objects accomplished, visions realized.

_____ Vision and Ideals

Serenity

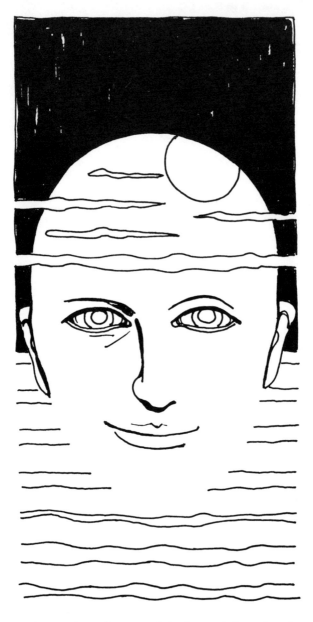

Peace of mind is one of the beautiful jewels of wisdom.

SERENITY

Peace of mind is one of the beautiful jewels of wisdom. It is the result of long and patient effort toward self-control. Its presence is a sign of matured experience, and of a more-than-ordinary knowledge of the laws and operations of thought.

Individuals become calm to the extent that they understand themselves to be beings who evolved from thought, for such knowledge requires the understanding that others developed as a result of the same process.

Secure, calm people are always loved and
respected. They are like shade-giving trees in a
desert....

And as they gain this understanding, and see more and more clearly the internal relations of things, they cease to complain, worry and grieve, and learn to live secure, dedicated and serene.

Those who are calm, having learned how to manage themselves, know how to adapt themselves to others. And those others, in turn, admire their spiritual strength, and feel that they can learn from them; and therefore, rely upon them. The more tranquil you become, the greater is your success, your influence, your power for good. Businessmen and women will see their prosperity increase as they develop greater self-control and composure, for everyone prefers to deal with persons of an even temper.

Secure, calm people are always loved and respected. They are like a shade-giving tree in a desert, or a sheltering cave in a storm. Who does

Keep your hands firmly upon the wheel of thought.

not love a peaceful heart, a sweet-tempered, balanced life? Through rain, shine and all kinds of changes, such persons are always sweet, serene and calm. That flawless facet of character, which we call serenity, is the last lesson of enrichment; it is the flowering of life, the harvest of the soul. It is as precious as wisdom, to be more desired than even gold. How insignificant the possession of mere money appears compared to serenity of soul—a life lived beyond the reach of storm, in the bosom of Eternal Calm.

How many people do you know who sour their lives, ruining everything that is sweet and beautiful by explosive tempers. It is perhaps true that the great majority of people destroy their lives and mar their happiness by lack of self-control. By contrast, how rare is the person who is in possession of that exquisite calmness which is the mark of a mature personality.

Humanity is filled with uncontrolled passion, racked with agonizing grief, and riddled with anxiety and doubt. Only the wise—the self-controlled—are able to make the storm winds of the soul obey.

Typhoon-tossed souls, wherever you are, under whatever conditions you live, know this—somewhere on the ocean of life the golden isles are smiling, and the sunny shore of your Ideal awaits your coming. Keep your hand firmly upon the wheel of thought. In the depth of your soul resides the Eternal Master. You are but asleep—awaken! Self-control is strength; Right Thought is mastery; Calmness is power. Say to your heart, "Peace, be still!"

FINIS

_____ Serenity

ABOUT THE ILLUSTRATOR

Kae Campbell is a professional graphic designer, illustrator and writer. She studied at the American Academy of Art in Chicago during the 1970's, and has since made her living doing commercial art for an eclectic group of clients. She has illustrated everything from children's books to double-decker beds, working in full color and black and white.

A serious painter, Kae is a member of the Chicago Artists Coalition. In fine art, she prefers abstract to representational, and works in gouache and acrylics. She has also written and published short stories and poems.

Ms. Campbell considers herself a full-time student in the school of life, with "degrees" in self-improvement, comparative religions, new age thinking, and an honorary "degree" in Survivalship. In this, she feels herself no more or no less privileged than others she has known along the way, and hopes to know through the pages of this book.

In approaching the illustrations for *As You Thinketh*, Kae decided to treat each design as a visual poem—trying to catch the sometimes elusive intangible—and make a visual statement. Fortunately, the author, James Allen, expressed himself so well with vivid word imagery, that the pictures leaped from the pages.

Coming Soon:
James Allen's
Unknown Books

POVERTY TO POWER
THE WAY OF PEACE
THE PATHWAY TO PROSPERITY

Revised and Updated
by Dr. Tag Powell

Top Of The Mountain Publishing
is dedicated to the expansion of
human potential.

For a FREE catalog of books and tapes
write:

FREE Catalog, Write, Phone or Fax
TOP OF THE MOUNTAIN PUBLISHING
BOX 2244 PINELLAS PARK, FL 33780-2244
Fax 813 391-4598 - Tel 813 391-3958
Web Site HTTP://ABCINFO.COM